I dedicate this book to my sister, Rosemary.
Thank you for your magical drawings,
sharing your talent and supporting me
in everything I do.
Love you, Carmen

I dedicate this book to my sister, Carmen!!
Thank you for being my lifelong guide,
and soulmate and for sharing your passion
for helping others with our talents.
I love you with all my heart.
Rosemary.

TWO tiny itsy bitsy GIFTS OF LIFE

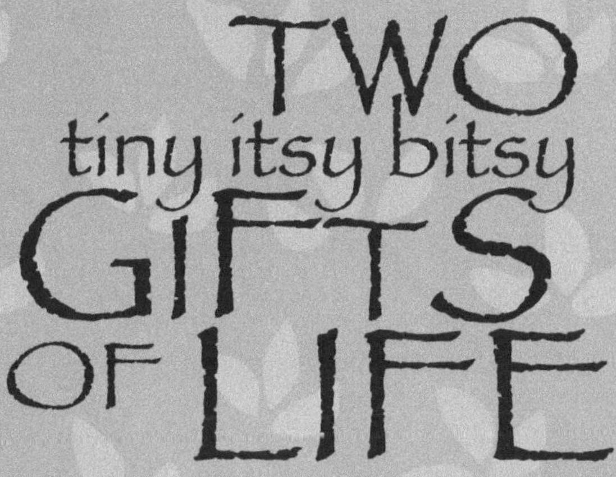

Written by
Carmen Martínez Jover

Illustrated by
Rosemary Martínez

Once upon a time there
were two monkeys:
Bowie and Tina.

They lived very happily
in their beautiful tree.

They loved swinging
from the trees
together and always
saw lots of little
monkeys everywhere,
but they didn't have
one of their own.

"Let's see,"
said Bowie,
"to make a baby
monkey we need a
tiny itsy bitsy egg
from you and a tiny
itsy bitsy sperm
from me."

"I really want us to
have our own baby
monkey," said Tina.

Yes, so do I,"
replied Bowie.
"I can't wait until
we become a
Mummy and Daddy."

But, Spring went by...

and Autumn went by...

and Summer went by…

and Winter went by…

and Tina
and Bowie had still
not become
a Mummy
and Daddy.

The doctor told Tina her tiny itsy bitsy eggs
weren't working and the doctor told
Bowie his tiny itsy bitsy sperms weren't
working either.

They both felt very sad.

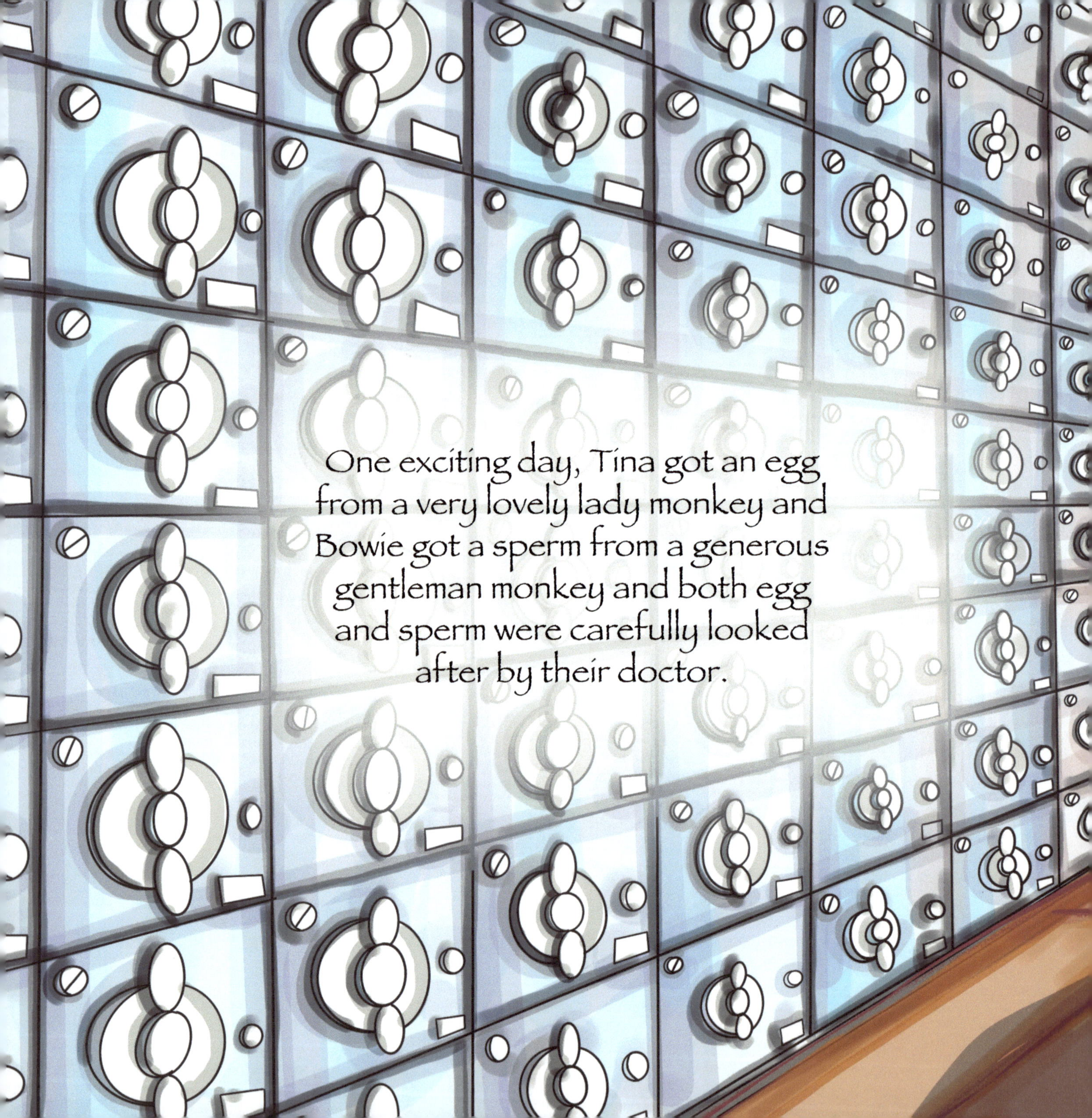

One exciting day, Tina got an egg
from a very lovely lady monkey and
Bowie got a sperm from a generous
gentleman monkey and both egg
and sperm were carefully looked
after by their doctor.

Tina and Bowie
treasured the tiny
itsy bitsy egg and the
tiny itsy bitsy sperm
because they needed
them in order to have
their own
baby monkey.

In the clinic, the doctor gently put Tina's
tiny itsy bitsy donated egg and Bowie's
tiny itsy bitsy donated sperm together
in a test tube and patiently looked after
them until they fertilised and became one,
forming an embryo, which is the beginning
of a baby monkey.

When the embryo started to grow, the
doctor placed it carefully into Tina's
womb, where it continued to grow.

Soon Tina's tummy
started to grow and
grow and grow.

Bowie would always
look after her.

Tina liked eating lots
of delicious things so
that the baby monkey
inside her tummy could
grow healthy
and strong.

They started preparing their baby monkey's bedroom.

It was such a lovely room.

Finally, Tina and Bowie
became a Mummy and Daddy!

Baby monkey was born and
do you know what?
Laby was the most beautiful
baby monkey
you have ever seen.

Laby grew...
and grew...
and grew...
and they lived happily ever after
as a family.

Be the **heroes** of **your** own **story.**

Personalise
your own story
with your own names.

http://www.fertilitybooks.net
https://books.carmenmartinezjover.com

SINGLE MUM BY CHOICE

Forever together, a single mum by choice story
for one child or twins.

ADOPTION

Soul's time to be born,
an adoption story.

Other books by: Rosemary & Carmen Martinez Jover

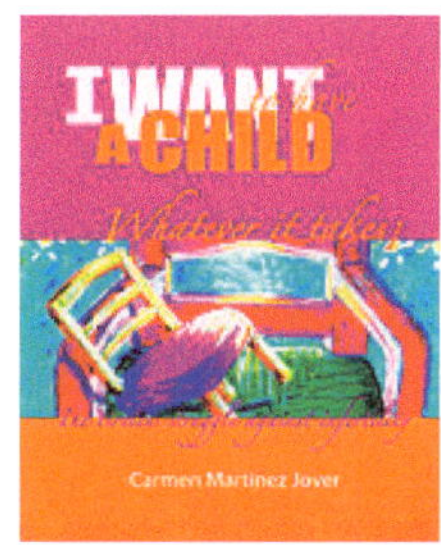

I want to have a child,
whatever it takes!

Recipes of How Babies
are Made

Bloom, wherever you may
be planted